RIDEAU CENTENNIAL SCHOOL
Portland, Ontario

THE FIRST CIVILIZATIONS

The First Civilizations

PETER
BEDRICK
BOOKS

This edition published in 2002 by Peter Bedrick Books
an imprint of McGraw-Hill Childrens's Publishing
8787 Orion Place,
Columbus, OH 43240

The material in this book has previously appeared in
History of the World (Bounty, Octopus Publishing Group Ltd, 2001)

ISBN 1-57768-950-X

Printed in China

**McGraw-Hill
Children's Publishing**

A Division of The **McGraw·Hill** *Companies*

PHOTOGRAPHIC CREDITS
32 (B/R) Robert Harding Picture Library; 45 (T/R) Bernard and Catherine Desjeux/CORBIS; 47
(T/R) Graham King. All other images from the Miles Kelly Archive.

QUOTATION ACKNOWLEDGEMENTS
Page 27 (translated by Frederick Morgan)published in *World Poetry* by W. W. Norton and Company; page
42, *The Iliad*, translated by Martin Hammond, published by Penguin Classics; page 45, *The Aeneid*, translated
by W.F. Jackson Knight, published by Penguin.

Every effort has been made to trace all copyright holders and obtain permissions. The editor and publishers
sincerely apologize for any inadvertent errors or omissions and will be happy to correct them in future edi-
tions.

Contents

The beginning of human history can be traced back long before the first human beings appeared – to the earliest forms of life on Earth about 3 billion years ago. Of the enormous variety of animals that evolved over millions of years, among the most advanced were tree-living mammals called primates. These included the first apes.

The First Humans

About 10 million years ago, some apes left the trees to walk on the open plains. They had large brains and used their fingers to pick up food. About 4 million years ago, the humanlike ape *Australopithecus* (southern ape) lived in Africa. It probably used sticks or stones as tools, in the same way that chimpanzees do.

The first humans
The first human species was *Homo habilis* (handy man), who lived in East Africa 2 million years ago. By 1.5 million years ago, the more advanced *Homo erectus*

(upright man) had appeared, and by 500,000 years ago, *Homo erectus* had learned to make fire. The first humans lived in family groups. They communicated in some form of language and worked together gathering plants and hunting animals for food.

Modern humans

About 400,000 years ago, a new species, more like us and known to scientists as *Homo sapiens* (wise man), had become the dominant human species. These humans made tools from stone and other materials. This "stone age" lasted until about 10,000 years ago, although isolated groups of people continued using stone tools until the present day.

In a series of migrations, humans spread to every continent. They crossed over land bridges, which were uncovered as seawater turned to ice during the Ice Age. People moved in groups from Africa across Europe and Asia, and into America and Australasia. Their social organization and developing technology helped them survive the harsh climate of the Ice Age.

Hunters become farmers

About 10,000 years ago, people became farmers for the first time. They planted crops and kept goats, cattle, and sheep. The earliest centers of the farming revolution were in the Near East and Asia. Here, people first settled in towns and developed a new way of life – the beginnings of civilization.

The first modern human was *Homo sapiens* (meaning "wise man"), who appeared between 400,000 and 300,000 years ago. His body looked like ours, but he had a large brain and small jaws. His limbs were longer and straighter than those of earlier people.

The First People

The ape-humans had used tools that were simply pebbles picked up from the ground. *Homo sapiens* were much more skillful, choosing stones with care. They chipped or flaked off bits to make shaped tools including hand axes, choppers, knives, and scrapers. These people also made use of other materials, such as animal bones and horns. The new humans spread from Africa into new territories. Several early forms of *Homo sapiens* seem to have lived in Africa, the Near East, and Asia. By about 35,000 years ago, they had reached Europe and Australia.

Neanderthals

In Europe, there was another human species, known as Neanderthal man, who for a time lived alongside modern humans. Scientists think Neanderthals were an "offshoot" of *Homo sapiens*, who adapted to life in the cold climates of the last Ice Age.

Neanderthal people lived in Europe from about 100,000 to 35,000 years ago. They took shelter in caves,

Early modern human (Homo sapiens) appears.	*c.* 350,000 BC
Neanderthal people appear.	*c.* 120,000 BC
Modern human (Homo sapiens sapiens) appears.	*c.* 100,000 BC
Modern humans spread to Europe and later to Australia.	*c.* 40,000 BC
Cro-Magnons appear in Europe.	*c.* 33,000 BC
Neanderthals either die out or are interbred into modern human populations.	*c.* 30,000 BC
Hunters roam Europe. Cave paintings are made.	*c.* 13,000 BC
Latest date for people to reach America from Asia.	*c.* 11,000 BC

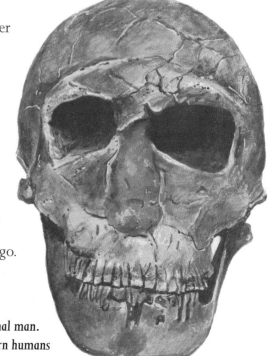

▷ *The large skull of a Neanderthal man. These people lived alongside modern humans during the last Ice Age.*

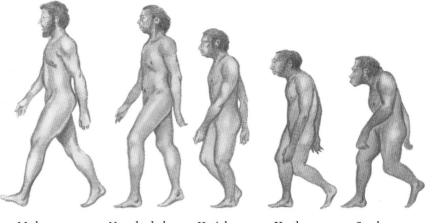

▷ Early peoples gradually looked less like humanoid apes and more like human beings. Bodies became more suited to walking upright, and legs became longer than arms.

Modern man Neanderthal man Upright man Handy man Southern ape

△ Stone Age people hunted with bows, spears, and flint axes. On the American grasslands, groups of hunters drove large grazing animals, such as mastodons and giant bison, to extinction.

made fire, and hunted animals, using stone tools and wooden spears. Although they had large brains, the heavily built Neanderthals were slower moving and less adaptable than the newcomers who started moving into Europe about 40,000 years ago. The Neanderthals were either wiped out by competition from other groups or integrated into humanity through interbreeding.

Cro-Magnons

The newcomers in Europe were the Cro-Magnons, who are named after the site in France where a group of their skeletons was discovered in 1868. Their bone structure was very similar to ours today. Cro-Magnons were probably our direct ancestors. Neanderthals and modern humans may have lived side by side and even bred between themselves. Yet it was the Cro-Magnons who won the evolutionary race.

The Stone Age

Historians call this period of prehistory the Stone Age, because stone was the most important material used by the first tool-makers. These early stone-crafting techniques show surprising skill.

Neanderthal burial

Neanderthals were the first humans to bury the dead. Archaeologists have found evidence of Neanderthal burial ceremonies. The remains of tools and meat have been found in graves, showing that the dead were buried with care.

Hand axe

Scraper

Spear head

△ Stone Age tools. Both the hand axe and scraper were made from flint. Spear heads were shaped from deer antlers. The hand axe was probably the most important early Stone Age tool.

From Africa, humans began to spread to every continent – a process that took almost 1 million years. Everywhere, humans were on the move. This was the age of the great migrations.

The Great Migrations

The Neanderthals vanished from Europe, although small groups may have remained in remote places. Modern humans moved across Europe and Asia and started to explore America and Australia. A wetter climate over the entire world produced a green region of lakes and grasslands in what is now the Sahara Desert. Animals and people thrived in these surroundings.

Cro-Magnons move into Europe from the Near East.	c. 38,000 BC
People reach America and Australia from Asia.	c. 33,000 BC
Neanderthals die out.	c. 28,000 BC
Evidence of cave people in Brazil.	c. 23,000 BC
Last wet period in Saharan North Africa.	c. 13,000 BC
People reach the tip of South America.	c. 8,000 BC
British Isles cut off by rising sea levels.	c. 3,000 BC
People reach Pacific Islands by boat.	c. 2,000 BC

Nomads, or wanderers, moved constantly to find fresh food supplies. Small groups of people walked across continents, following the animals they hunted for food.

Some moved into the north of Asia and even traveled across to what is now Alaska, but most of these early peoples on the move headed toward warmer regions. They began to settle on grassy plains and close to water. Everyone lived in harmony with nature, and their lives were regulated by the seasons.

We can form an idea of what early human life was like from studies of the Australian Aborigines. Until the 18th century, these people had little contact with the world beyond Australia. A few isolated groups of people in parts of

△ *Aboriginal rock artists looked "beneath the skin" to show a person's bones or organs. Paintings of people and animals are found at sites linked in Aboriginal belief to the Dream Time, when spirits created the world.*

Making fires

People made fire using a simple wooden stick called a fire drill. The drill was turned quickly over a piece of dry wood until it produced enough heat to start the fire.

South America and Southeast Asia also preserved a "Stone Age" way of life into the modern age.

The Aborigines

The Aborigines probably reached Australia overland, crossing a land bridge that joined New Guinea to Australia 30,000 years ago. They had boats, so sea migrations were also possible. There is also a theory that some crossed the Pacific Ocean and landed in America.

Food, clothes, and tools

These people lived by gathering food and hunting. Along the coast, they fished with nets, basket traps, and spears. In the bush, they used fire to drive animals into traps and made poisons from leaves and roots to drug fish in pools. Women and children collected roots, fruits, insects, and honey from wild bees' nests. They wore no clothes and rubbed animal fats onto their bodies to protect themselves from cold.

Technology was simple. The Aborigines made simple stick shelters. They made stone tools and knew how to use bows and arrows as well as spear-throwing. The boomerang was used for hunting and war.

Paintings and dances

On rocks and cave walls, artists used colored earth to make paintings, telling stories of myths and legends. This rock art, and the songs and dances of the people, reveals spiritual beliefs. One of the most powerful beliefs was the notion of the "Dream Time" – this was the time when all living things were created.

△ *Stone Age hunters killed deer and other animals with spears, bows, and stones, often ambushing a herd on the move. The humans' intelligence, weapons, and teamwork made up for their comparative lack of strength and speed.*

△ *The Aborigines used ritual boomerangs, decorated with secret symbols, in magical dances.*

BC

400,000
100,000
20,000
10,000
4,000
2,000

Around 18,000 years ago, the last of a series of Ice Ages gripped much of the Northern Hemisphere. Icecaps spread southward across Europe and North America. The sea level fell, uncovering land bridges which animals and people had crossed – between Asia and Alaska for example.

The Last Ice Age

Hunters make clay figures of people and animals. — c. 23,000 BC

Cave dwellers made paintings about this time at Lascaux in France and Altamira in Spain. — c. 23,000 BC

Last Ice Age reaches its coldest point. Earliest rock art known in Asia. — c. 16,000 BC

Hunter-gatherers cross from Asia into North America via the exposed Bering Strait. — c. 14,000 BC

End of the last Ice Age. Possible first domestic animal - the dog - used for hunting. — c. 11,000 BC

New Stone Age begins. — c. 6,000 BC

This last Ice Age had a dramatic effect on people's way of life. The spread of snow and ice reduced the size of the areas in which they could live. Many moved away to seek warmer regions. Other groups adapted to living in the freezing conditions. Clothed only in animal skins and taking shelter in caves and tents, people tried to survive around the fringes of the vast ice sheets.

Tool-making

People who kept themselves alive by hunting needed good weapons and tools. They made these from flints, choosing stones that were easily chipped or flaked to create useful cutting and scraping edges. Where good flints were found, people dug mines to hack out the stones. They set up tool-making "factories" where they made polished stone axes and other tools with great skill.

▷*As well as being an important source of meat, woolly mammoths provided skins for clothing and shelter. Their bones and tusks were carved into tools and decorative ornaments.*

12

▷ Cave artists used natural paints made from colored earth and plant juices. Their drawings may have been made for ritual magic, to bring success to a group's hunters.

△ This Ice Age man is using a stone blade to scrape clean the skin of a hunted animal.

Tool-makers settled near their mines and traded their finished tools with other groups. The first trade routes were made by people traveling from one place to another to exchange goods. In boggy areas, the first "roads" were made – consisting of wooden walkways built from logs. Near rivers and lakes, people became skilled boatmen and fishermen, making their craft from hollowed-out tree trunks and bundles of reeds. They wove fishing nets and built lakeside huts on stilts. They made fire with friction (rubbing) techniques, using a bowdrill or striking flints. Once a fire was lit, people did their best to make sure it did not go out.

Social life

People living in groups had to find ways of working together. They developed ideas of sharing tasks between men and women, and between individuals. Expert tool-makers (perhaps women or the elderly) stayed in camp while others went hunting – and so had more time to practice their skills for the benefit of the group.

By working together, early humans were able to hunt and kill big animals such as mammoth and bison.

Hut of mammoth bones

Ice Age hunters made shelters from the bones of mammoths. They made the framework of bones and filled in the gaps with skins, turf, and moss. Groups of men drove the animals into swamps, where they became trapped and were killed with spears or rocks.

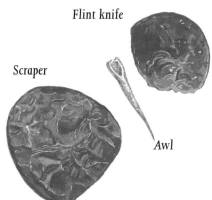

Flint knife

Scraper

Awl

△ Tools for scraping were made mainly from flint. This hard material could be chipped into tools of many different shapes and sizes. Other tools were made from bone, antlers, and tusks.

BC

400,000
100,000
20,000
10,000
4,000
2,000

About 10,000 years ago the icecap had shrunk. Warmer weather made life much easier and human groups began to grow. In places, people who used to wander around looking for food found that, by gathering wild cereal plants such as rice and wheat, and sowing the seeds, they could grow new plants in the same place.

The First Farmers

People naturally chose plants with the largest grain-heads. A chance cross-breeding of wheat and wild grass in the Jordan Valley in Israel produced a new wheat with bigger grains. People found that grinding the grains produced flour, the basic ingredient in bread, an important new food. How this breakthrough in skill and diet happened is not clear, but it changed history.

Sheep may have been domesticated.	*c.* 9,000 BC
Start of farming in the Near East. Walls of Jericho, the earliest town, built.	*c.* 8,000 BC
Wheat and barley are grown in the Near East. Pigs and cattle are domesticated.	*c.* 7,000 BC
Farming spreads west into Europe and east into Asia. Copper in use. Pottery made.	*c.* 6,000 BC
First use of brick for building in the Near East.	*c.* 5,000 BC
First farmers cross to Britain. First plows used in Near East.	*c.* 4,000 BC
Invention of the wheel in Mesopotamia. Use of copper tools spreads.	*c.* 3,500 BC
Domestication of the horse in central Asia.	*c.* 2,500 BC

Settling down
People no longer wandered after herds of wild animals or in search of fresh plants to pick. Instead, some stayed in one place, making homes beside their new plots of roughly tilled and sown ground. They had become farmers.

Rivers and lakes were good places to settle. Fish could be caught in nets and water channeled along ditches to the new fields. The first farmers made new tools, such as wooden digging sticks and sickles with flint blades, to harvest their crops. Farmers tamed animals too. Hunters had already tamed wolf cubs to help in the hunt, but now

Populations grew after the Ice Age. People could not find enough food by the old way of hunting and gathering. A new strategy was needed to survive: farming and the raising of domestic animals.

△ Early tools were made from materials such as flint, bone, and antlers. Common ones were the flint sickle (right), the flint and wood hammer (center), and the antler pick (left).

◁ The first farmers made their own homes, clothing, and tools. In a good year, their crops gave them more food than they needed, so they traded this surplus with neighbors. They also had domestic animals.

domestic dogs were trained to herd flocks of sheep and goats. Farm animals were bred from young wild animals, captured and raised among people. Domesticated animals were then bred to make them more docile and suitable for human use.

Farmers and new tools

The first farmers lived in the Near East, across a region stretching west from the Nile Valley to the Tigris and Euphrates rivers. This area became known as the Fertile Crescent. Farming also developed in other continents at this time – in China and in the Americas.

With farming came new inventions and skills. People made pottery and invented the wheel, used first to turn the clay as it was shaped. They made metal tools, first from cold-beaten copper (about 8,500 years ago), then from bronze (a mixture of copper and tin formed by heat). About 5,000 years ago, people learned how to smelt (melt and separate) iron ore from rocks. They used the iron to make tools, both for peace and for war.

Iron Age world

Farming brought new wealth. Trade grew as did warfare. The richer people clustered together to defend themselves against raids by envious enemies. Village life demanded a communal form of government. Chieftains who had once led bands of nomads became rulers of villages. Some of the villages grew rapidly into the world's first towns.

△ The first farmers began to develop new skills, which included the use of fire to make metal tools and weapons. The tools seen here are (from left to right): a sickle for harvesting crops, a knife, and a pair of pincers.

15

Civilization began with the first towns. Towns grew into cities, which became the centers of the world's first empires. Egypt, the Indus Valley, and China all had advanced societies.

The First Civilizations

Impressive civilizations also rose in central America, Africa south of the Sahara, and the eastern Mediterranean. Religion, trade, art, and lawmaking developed. So did technology – and warfare. Human life became more organized and complex.

The first towns
The oldest known town ruins are those of Jericho – its walls date from about 11,000 years ago. The ruins of Catal Huyuk, in Turkey, date from about 8,250 years ago. People built towns in Mesopotamia, Egypt, the Indus Valley, China, and Central America. Rivers were the cradles of these new civilizations, attracting farmers and traders. Towns became marketplaces, and cities became centers of government.

Kings and cities
The early city-states were led by kings, who made laws. Often kings were also priests. Powerful kings such as Sargon of Akkad

and Hammurabi of Babylon ruled the first empires. The pharaohs of Egypt lived in imperial splendor, in a land made rich by farming and trade. Other rulers built luxurious palaces such as Knossos on the island of Crete.

The period from 5,000 BC to 500 BC produced magnificent buildings, such as the ziggurats of Babylon and the pyramids of Egypt. The stones of Stonehenge and the mysterious heads left by the Olmecs in Central America show that people in Europe and America were also artists and builders.

New technology and ideas

This was an age of crucial new technologies – the wheel, metal tools, and weapons were developed at this time. Coins were first used. Writing and mathematics developed. The Babylonians studied the stars. New ideas were evolving, and spreading with the help of trade, ready to shape the next stage of human history.

BC

400,000
100,000
20,000
10,000
2,000
4,000

When people settled down to farm they chose to live near a water supply, often a river. Between two mighty rivers – the Tigris and the Euphrates in Mesopotamia – the world's first great civilization rose 6,000 years ago.

Mesopotamia

Mesopotamia, meaning "between rivers," lay in the country we know as modern Iraq. Northern Mesopotamia's weather was mild, with enough rain for crops to grow in some areas. In the south lay a flat, swampy plain built up from mud spread by the river floodwaters. This area was called Sumer. It had little rain and long, hot summers.

Sumer
People had lived in Sumer since 5,000 BC. They fished the rivers, hunted wild pigs and birds for food, and picked fruit from date palms. The muddy soil was rich, but crops died without rain in the burning summer heat. So farmers dug canals to channel river water to their fields of barley, wheat, dates, and vegetables. They turned over the earth with plows pulled by oxen.

Gods and grain
Farming flourished and by around 3,500 BC, new people settled in Sumer. With their arrival, cities began to grow. Food was plentiful, so farming villages grew in number and size. People lived and worked together. Their buildings of mud brick included a house – or temple – for the local god. Here they offered gifts in return for the god's care of

▷ People in Mesopotamia traded along the rivers, using small boats. By 5,000 years ago, people had invented the wheel, and carts were pulled by oxen and donkeys. Sacks of barley were traded as currency as well as being used for food.

c. 4,000 BC The weaving loom is in use by this date. Hot metal working in Near East.

c. 3,800 BC Earliest map on a clay tablet shows River Euphrates.

c. 3,500 BC Towns of Uruk (Eridu) and Ur in Sumer. First use of potter's wheel.

c. 3,500 BC Invention of the wheel in Mesopotamia. Flax grown to make linen.

c. 3,200 BC Cuneiform writing developed in Sumer.

c. 3,000 BC First city-states in Mesopotamia and Near East.

c. 2,500 BC Domestication of the horse in central Asia.

c. 2,000 BC Destruction of the city of Ur by the Elamites. The last king of Ur, Ibbi-Sin, is taken captive.

△ *Some of the wedge-shaped ("cuneiform") characters in the Sumerian writing system looked like objects; others were symbols.*

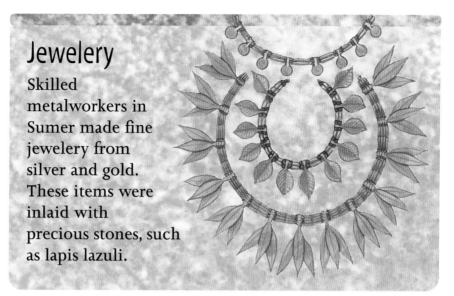

Jewelery

Skilled metalworkers in Sumer made fine jewelery from silver and gold. These items were inlaid with precious stones, such as lapis lazuli.

their families, homes, crops, and animals. Gifts of harvest crops led to the temple also being used as a grain store. Even farm animals such as oxen and donkeys were kept there, perhaps to hire out for work in the fields.

Writing and counting

Goods passing in and out of the temple store had to be checked and recorded. A system of numbers and counting was invented – as well as the world's first writing system. People skilled in writing, called scribes, were highly trained, important people.

The beginning of writing is also the beginning of human history. Sumerians used clay tablets and a sharpened reed to carve wedge-shaped characters into the soft, damp surface. The clay was baked hard, so the writing became a permanent record. Sumerian tablets can still be read. The Sumerian system of counting has lasted, too. They used units of 60 when telling the time in seconds, minutes, and hours and when measuring a circle with 360 degrees.

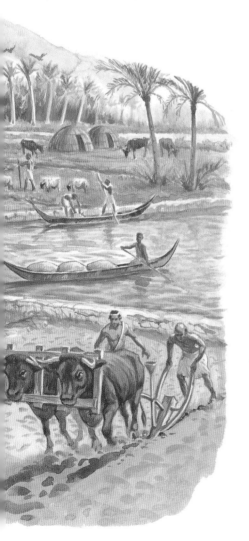

▷ *Sumerian women wore long dresses and robes. Rich women liked jewelery, such as bead necklaces, gold earrings, and headdresses.*

BC

400,000
100,000
20,000
10,000
4,000
2,000

Town life created a society with more rules in which more people did specialized tasks. The world of city-states such as Ur was one run largely by men.

Society and City-states

A man was master of his household, including his wife, children, and slaves. Women could, however, own their own property. Boys from wealthier families, such as the sons of court officials, went to school to be taught by scribes. Other children learned to do what their parents did at home.

First cities of Mesopotamia.	3,500 BC
Cities and temples in Sumer built of mud brick.	3,000 BC
Rise of city of Ur.	2,850 BC
Gilgamesh, legendary ruler.	2,750 BC
Rise of the Akkad Empire.	2,400 BC
Sargon of Akkad is first great king.	2,350 BC
King Ur-Nammu rules Ur.	2,112 BC
King Hammurabi rules Babylon.	1,750 BC

Priest power
Priests were important because of the temple trade. They organized everyone who worked in and around the temple, from craftworkers to merchants and scribes. Villagers farmed land for the gods, under the priests' watchful eyes. Farmers paid rent to the temple, and priests also acted as tax collectors. In return, a state allowance of food was distributed to city dwellers.

As villages grew into towns and cities, temple officials played a big part in ruling them. A rich and powerful elite class emerged, living in splendid temple-palaces. Most powerful of all was the king, the gods' representative on Earth. He was responsible for law and government, for keeping order, and for defending civilization against enemies.

City-states and their rulers
Among the earliest cities of southern Mesopotamia were Eridu, Uruk, Nippur, and Kish. These cities were like small states, with their own

▷ In Mesopotamia, there were hundreds of gods and goddesses, including Nanna the moon god and Inanna the goddess of love and war.

ENKI   NINHURSAG   NANNA   UTU   INANNA

◁ The royal standard of Ur, a decorated wooden box, dates from about 2,500 BC. On its mosaic panels, farmers parade and soldiers march into battle.

△ King Hammurabi of Babylon (ruled c.1792 −1750 BC) is shown before the sun god at the top of this carved stone pillar. The king's laws were carved onto the pillar below.

government and rulers. Around 2,700 BC, the title "lugal," meaning big man, was used for the ruler of Kish. Uruk, which in about 2,700 BC was the first city to protect itself with a wall, had a ruler with the title "En."

Sargon of Akkad

City-states often fought one another over trade and border disputes. Sumerian soldiers fought mainly on foot, although some rode in chariots drawn by wild donkeys (onagers). When one city grew powerful enough to rule the others, it created a small kingdom, such as those of Lagash and Ur. Around 2,375 BC, Lagash and all the other city-states of Sumer were defeated by Lugalzaggisi, ruler of Umma. Sumer was united under his rule for 25 years. But from the north came an even mightier conqueror – Sargon of Akkad – the first great king in history.

Sargon created the first empire in Mesopotamia. One of his successors, the fourth king of Akkad, was Naram-Sin (he reigned from 2,254 to 2,218 BC), whose war triumphs are recorded on a famous sculpture, the Naram-Sin Stele.

Sargon of Akkad

Sargon had been cup-bearer to the king of Kish. Records say that he fought the Sumerian cities, threw down city walls, and took 50 of their rulers captive, including the ruler of Uruk. Sargon ruled for a total of 56 years. He made one of his daughters a priestess of the moon god in Ur.

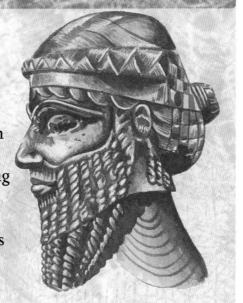

△ In the city-states of Mesopotamia, scribes such as the one shown here carved the local ruler's code of laws onto clay tablets.

BC

400,000
100,000
20,000
10,000
4,000
2,000

In Mesopotamia, as many as 300,000 people lived in a big city. Within the walls, the city was a maze of narrow streets, alleys, and marketplaces. Many buildings were made of mud brick but some houses were built from reeds. They were similar to those still used by people living in southern Iraq.

Homes and Temples

First cities of Mesopotamia.	3,500 BC
Writing in Sumer. First use of bronze.	3,200 BC
Cities and temples in Sumer built of mud brick.	3,000 BC
Great Pyramid of Giza built in Egypt.	2,590 BC

A well-to-do family lived in a two-story home with no windows. It had a flat roof where the family might sleep and a central courtyard that was pleasantly cool in the evening. Here, visitors would have their dusty feet washed by a slave. The bedrooms were upstairs; the kitchen, living room, and storerooms were downstairs. There was little furniture - only chests, stools, and tables – and most people slept on mats, although some rich people had beds. Each home had a shrine, set in the wall, and often a small family tomb.

Food and drink
The Sumerians made unleavened bread (bread that does not rise) and ate porridge made from wheat and barley grains. Vegetables, dates, milk, butter, and cheese were served at

▷ *A ziggurat consisted of an enormous platform structure with an earth core, over which unglazed bricks were laid. The building was faced with fire bricks. Ramps and steps led up to the top, where the temple was erected.*

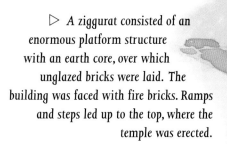

▷ Brick-makers fired bricks in kilns to produce building materials for structures that were intended to last. Kiln-fired bricks could survive the seasonal rains without needing too much repair.

mealtimes too. Cattle and sheep provided meat, and fish was a very popular food. Fish "take-out" stalls sold ready-cooked fish. The favorite drink was beer. For entertainment, people played board games, listened to stories of legendary heroes, or played musical instruments. Water and food were kept in large storage jars. Glass was made, some time before 2,000 BC, but for use in jewelery.

Temples to the gods

The Sumerians worshipped many gods and goddesses – gods of the sky, the air, the Sun, the Moon, fertility, and wisdom. Each city had its own patron god.

Slaves, taken captive in war, toiled to build Mesopotamia's splendid temples. The White Temple in Uruk, built in 3,000 BC, was made of whitewashed brick, set on top of a pyramid or ziggurat. A ziggurat was an artificial mountain, on which the people thought the local god lived, watching over the citizens he protected. The ziggurat's platform of earth was faced with bricks. Temples were built on top of the platform. The Hanging Gardens of Babylon, one of the Seven Wonders of the Ancient World, were probably built in the same way.

△ Reed houses were built using reeds cut down from the marshes around the Tigris and Euphrates rivers. The Sumerians also made canoes from these reeds.

The wheel

The wheel was first used by the Sumerians in making pottery in about 3,500 BC. About 300 years later, this invention was adapted for a startling new use – transportation.

△ Mud bricks, dried in the sun, were one of the least expensive building materials. These sun-dried bricks were made stronger with straw, but they were not waterproof.

After the fall of Ur in 2,000 BC, many cities of Mesopotamia were ruled by the Amorites, whose two strongholds were Isin and Larsa. In 1,763 BC, Larsa fell to a great army led by Hammurabi (1,792–1,750 BC). The new ruler gave the new name, Babylonia, to the kingdoms of Sumer and Akkad.

Babylonia

Under Hammurabi, all of Mesopotamia came under one rule. The king of Babylonia was also the high priest of the national god. The palace now held power over the temple. Under the king there were three classes of people: aristocrats, commoners, and slaves. Trade was no longer controlled by the city, so merchants and traders managed their own businesses.

The laws of Hammurabi

The laws of King Hammurabi applied across his empire. They covered trade, business and prices, family law, criminal law, and civil laws. Their main principle was "the strong shall not injure the weak." Hammurabi also set up a system of set prices and wages and gave his people a fair and well-run tax system. In AD 1901, his laws were found written on a stone slab in Susa, Iran where a victorious king had taken it as war booty.

One of the conflicts between the former

Hittites make iron tools and weapons.	2,000 BC
First Babylonian dynasty.	1,830 BC
Fall of Larsa. Hammurabi rules Babylon.	1,763 BC
Babylon conquers other city-states.	1,750 BC
Nebuchadnezzar fights off Assyrian invasion.	1,125 BC
Tiglath-pileser I of Assyria conquers Babylon.	1,116 BC
Babylon again invaded by Assyrians.	700s BC
Old Babylon falls.	689 BC
Rise of New Babylon.	626 BC

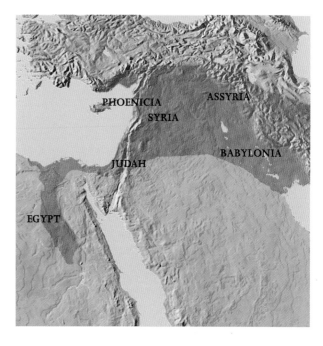

▷ This map shows the extent of the Babylonian Empire under King Nebuchadnezzar II. Under his rule, the Babylonians captured Syria and Palestine.

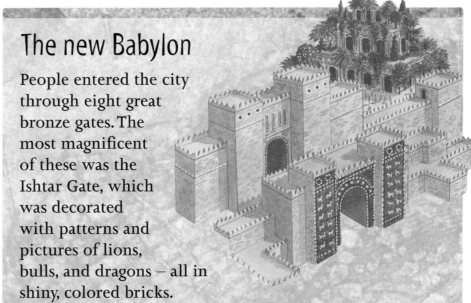

The new Babylon

People entered the city through eight great bronze gates. The most magnificent of these was the Ishtar Gate, which was decorated with patterns and pictures of lions, bulls, and dragons – all in shiny, colored bricks.

△ Marduk was the chief god of Babylonia. Poets praised him as kind and merciful lord of the heavens and the source of civilization and law. His sacred animals included the dragon.

states of Babylonia was over the control of river waters. In wartime, rulers dammed rivers to cause flood or drought in the land of their enemies. Sometimes a river would be diverted away from the crops of a rival city. Hammurabi now commanded the water power.

Hammurabi's city

The city of Babylon had magnificent temples and palaces. Its winding, narrow streets were lined with private houses. Most had a courtyard with rooms around it. In the city walls were gates, around which traders held markets. Traders and merchants traveled as far afield as Syria, Assyria, and the kingdoms of the Persian Gulf.

The fall of Babylon

During 700 BC, Assyrians from the upper Tigris area, north of Babylonia, invaded Babylon. The city was destroyed in 689 BC by the Assyrian king Sennacherib but later rebuilt. A new Babylonian empire began to grow in 626 BC, when the general Nabopolassae defeated the Assyrians. Under this king and his son, Nebuchadnezzar II, the Babylonian Empire controlled most of the Middle East.

△ The Babylonians produced written records by carving picture symbols onto clay tablets. The tablets carried information about astronomy and mathematics, as well as records of legal and business matters and religious texts.

▷ The ancient Babylonians were the first to study the stars, some time before 2,000 BC. They knew of five planets: Jupiter, Mars, Mercury, Saturn, and Venus.

The city-states of Sumer traded across the Arabian Sea with people who lived by another great river – the River Indus, which flows through Pakistan. Here, one of the world's first great civilizations had begun, like Sumer, with farms, villages, and small towns.

The Indus Valley

Around 2500 BC, cities were planned and built. These cities remained unknown until archaeologists began excavating them in the AD 1920s. There were two main cities – Harappa in the north of the Indus Valley and Mohenjo Daro in the south. The people who lived here were farmers, tending fields and watering crops with silt-laden waters washed down when the snows melted in the mountains to the north.

Well-planned cities

Harappa and Mohenjo Daro were carefully planned and laid out on a grid system. They were large cities, over 3 miles around their outer boundary. The cities had wide roads and brick houses, most of which

Farming settlements grow in the Indus Valley.	3000 BC
First cities of the Indus Valley.	2500 BC
Aryans from the north begin to threaten Indus peoples.	2100 BC
Indus Valley civilization begins to decline.	2000 BC
Indus Valley civilization is destroyed.	1500 BC

▷ The city of Harappa. Many houses were built on mud-brick platforms to save them from seasonal floods. Most had baths, with water from a public well or a well in the courtyard.

Priest kings

Rulers known as priest kings were found in all the great ancient civilizations. This ruler was the link between people and god, on whose will their fate depended. Both Harappa and Mohenjo Daro were probably ruled by a priest king and by a priestly elite.

△ Archaeologists have found hundreds of artifacts during the excavation of Mohenjo Daro. Many, such as this bronze figurine of a dancing girl, have been well preserved in the sand and mud around the settlement.

△ The farmers of the Indus Valley used wooden carts pulled by a pair of oxen. Deep grooves made by heavily laden carts have been found in the excavated streets of Mohenjo Daro.

had at least two floors. The standards of hygiene and sanitation were high. Many houses had private bathrooms, with pipes leading to main drains under the streets. People also used public wells and baths. Bathing may have been part of certain religious rituals, for which the Great Bath found at Mohenjo Daro probably had a religious function.

Traders used a standard system of weights and measures, and each city had a large granary stocked with grain. Farmers grew wheat, barley, peas, mustard, sesame seeds, dates, and cotton. Domesticated animals included dogs, cats, cattle, chickens and possibly pigs, camels, buffalo, and elephants. Over 100 other towns and villages have been found in the Indus Valley.

Rich from trade

All this suggests a high level of organization. Temples were smaller and less impressive than those of Mesopotamia, but the people of the Indus Valley enjoyed clean and well-run cities. Food was their main export, and trade was carried on by ship with copper producers in the Persian Gulf. Caravans from the north brought silver from Afghanistan and lead from Rajasthan. There was also trade with Sumer, and similarities in art found suggest the two cultures copied each other's fashions.

" No thing existed, nor did nothing exist:/ there was no air-filled space, no sky beyond./ What held it all? And where? And who secured it?

from THE RIG VEDA, c. 1,500 BC

The Rig Veda is a religious song about the ancient gods of fire, earth, air, and water.

BC

400,000
100,000
20,000
10,000
4,000
2,000

The first great civilization in Europe arose in Greece, around 3,000 BC, on the island of Crete in the Mediterranean Sea. It was named "Minoan" after the legendary King Minos of Crete. In Greek myths, Minos was the son of Europa and Zeus, the king of the gods.

Crete and Mycenae

The Cretans were among the first people to make bronze tools and weapons. They were farmers and fishing people who lived in small towns or villages protected not by walls or forts but by the sea. These seafarers were the first naval power known in history.

Sailors and traders

The Cretans sailed the Aegean and Mediterranean seas in ships laden with goods produced by the island's farmers and skilled craftworkers – pottery, engraved stone seals, perfumes, metalwork, woolen textiles, olive oil, wine, grain, and grapes. Minoan pottery found its way to Egypt, where tomb paintings show Cretans bringing gifts for the pharaoh. They carried tin, gold, pearls, and ivory back to Crete. Trade made the Minoans wealthy.

Palace of Knossos

The chief town of Crete was Knossos, where the ruler lived in a luxurious hilltop palace. Courtyards, storehouses, and workshops formed part of the palace, which was also the center of government and an important grain store.

Earliest settlements on Crete.	c. 6000 BC
Stone-built villages on coasts of Crete. Trade with Egypt and Anatolia.	c. 3000 BC
Minoan Crete at height of its power. Palace at Knossos.	2000 BC
Start of Mycenean power. Mycenae becomes an important center.	1900 BC
Mycenae rivals the Minoans of Crete.	1500 BC
Volcanic explosion on island of Thera in Aegean Sea.	1470 BC
Myceneans take over Crete. Knossos is destroyed by fire.	1400 BC
Lion gate at Mycenae built.	1300 BC
Collapse of Mycenean civilization.	c. 1,150 BC

▷ The so-called "mask of Agamemnon" was found during the excavation of graves at Mycenae in the late 1800s. Modern historians think the mask belonged to an earlier king.

△ *The Minoans favored goddesses in their worship, including the snake goddess who protected the home. The Cretan civilization left behind a rich legacy of religious beliefs and tales of heroes and gods.*

△ *Both the Cretans and the Myceneans had forms of writing, which they used in business and government. They wrote on clay tablets and possibly also in ink on papyrus, like the Egyptians. We know of two forms of writing, or scripts, called Linear A and Linear B.*

The Minotaur

According to legend, King Minos kept a half-human, half-bull called the Minotaur in his palace at Knossos. Wall paintings there show young acrobats leaping along bulls' backs.

By about 1580 BC, Minoan civilization was spreading to other Aegean islands and to the mainland of Greece. There were palaces in other Minoan towns, such as Mallia and Phaisos. The great palace at Knossos, crushed by an earthquake in 1700 BC, had risen again in even grander form. In about 1450 BC, another earthquake hit Crete. After this, the Myceneans – a people from mainland Greece – ruled the island.

Mycenean warriors

The Myceneans were warlike people who lived in Greece, possibly from 1900 BC. By 1600 BC, they were trading in the Aegean, and, after the fall of Crete, they became the major power in the region. They had settlements from Sicily to Syria and close links with Troy, a city in the rich grain-growing area at the mouth of the Black Sea.

The Mycenean rulers lived in hilltop citadels overlooking cities protected by thick stone walls. The city of Mycenae was at the heart of their civilization. People entered Mycenae through the Lion Gate, a great stone gateway from which a path led straight to the royal palace. Graves of the ruling family, filled with treasure and personal possessions for the afterlife, were found near the gate in AD 1876.

By 1100 BC, Mycenean power was over. Raids by pirates cut off Mediterranean trade routes from the Greek mainland. Weakened by interstate warfare, the Mycenean cities were destroyed and lost.

◁ *Like other Minoan palaces, the palace at Knossos was designed for elegant living and day-to-day business. Short wooden columns supported the decorated beams of the ceiling.*

BC
400,000
100,000
20,000
10,000
4,000
2,000

None of the civilizations in western Europe could rival those of Egypt and the Near East. However, more than 5,000 years ago Europeans were building spectacular stone monuments. Many of these are still standing today, as mysterious relics of a long-gone society.

Megalithic Europe

First stone structures in Europe.	4,500 BC
Passage graves built at Carnac in France.	4,000 BC
Lake villages in central Europe.	3,000 BC
Stone temples on the island of Malta.	2,800 BC
Beaker Folk begin to settle in Britain.	2,500 BC
End of New Stone Age in Britain. First use of bronze.	2,000 BC
Earliest work at Stonehenge.	1,800 BC
Stonehenge is more or less complete.	1,400 BC
Celts begin to settle in Britain.	1,000 BC

The huge stones of these monuments are called megaliths (meaning "big stones"). Some were set up on their own, others in groups or in circles. Some megaliths marked the burial place of an important ruler, while others seem to have had a religious meaning.

Europe's population grew as farming developed. People in the north looked southward towards the Mediterranean for new ideas. Traders from the civilized southern world came as far north as Britain, in search of tin needed to make bronze.

Most Europeans lived in small villages, ruled by a chieftain. His power was based on the number of weapons, sheep, and cattle he owned. Chieftains controlled trade and the places where people met to do business – river fords, valleys, and forest clearings where trails crossed. Travel was difficult because there were no proper roads. Clumsy ox-drawn wagons with iron-rimmed wheels creaked slowly along, carrying heavy goods.

The settlement of Britain

Before 3000 BC, few people lived in the British Isles apart from scattered groups of wandering hunters. Then, farmers and herders from

△ Stonehenge was built in stages between 1800 and 1400 BC. During the second stage, blue stones from the Preseli Mountains in Wales were hauled onto the site in an astonishing feat of organization and transport. Local stones added in the third stage weighed up to 55 tons.

Stone relics

Rock tombs, slab tombs such as this dolmen (right) and stone circles and temples lie scattered across Europe, even on the island of Malta. The work of trimming and raising the stones required skill.

△ Many people in Britain and Europe lived in village communities. A typical village dwelling consisted of a round wooden framework, filled in with twigs, turf, and mud, and a thatched roof.

mainland Europe arrived. They brought cattle, sheep, and pigs, and began to clear the forests to grow crops.

From about 2500 BC, new migrants arrived, bringing with them bronze tools and a distinctive pottery. Historians call them the "Beaker Folk." They mined copper and tin, made gold jewelery, and wove wool and linen for clothing.

Mound diggers and stone movers

People had no machines, and yet they tackled large digging works. They buried their chieftains, with treasures and food for the next world, beneath mounds of earth called "barrows." Many of these barrows can still be seen.

Tall single stones (menhirs), stone slab-tombs (dolmens), and the remains of large circles of stones and wooden posts (henges) are also still standing. In Britain, the most impressive stone circles are at Avebury and Stonehenge in Wiltshire. At Carnac, in northern France, there are avenues of standing stones.

Iron Age Europe

The Stonehenge builders had only stone or bronze tools. The Iron Age began in central Europe about 1000 BC. Early iron-using people mined salt as well as iron ore. About 1000 BC, new settlers called Celts came to Britain from mainland Europe. These newcomers were iron-makers and fort-builders.

▷ The Celts were skilled craftworkers, making highly decorated ornaments from bronze and iron. Their work featured elaborate and distinctive patterns of interwoven curves and spirals.

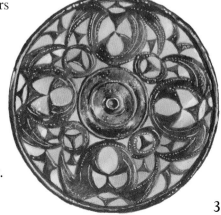

BC

400,000

100,000

20,000

10,000

2,000

4,000

For most of a period lasting 3,000 years, Egypt was the strongest power in the world. It ruled an empire which, at its peak in about 1500 BC, included Palestine and Syria. Egyptians kings, or pharaohs, built the greatest monuments of the ancient world – the Pyramids.

Egypt

Egyptian armies fought off invaders and conquered new lands, while traders journeyed across the Mediterranean Sea and southward into Africa to bring back treasures to add to Egypt's wealth. This wealth was based on the mighty Nile River. The Egyptians called their land Kemet ("black land"). Each year, the Nile flooded and its waters spilled over the banks to spread a layer of black, fertile mud on the fields where the farmers grew their crops. This yearly gift of the Nile allowed people to enjoy a civilization of plenty.

First dynastic period. Egypt is united under one king.	3,100 BC
Old Kingdom. The Pyramids are built at Giza.	2,686– 2,160 BC
A period of unrest and famine. Pyramids are robbed.	2,160– 2,040 BC
Middle Kingdom. Capital of Egypt moves to Thebes. Strong pharaohs rule.	2,040– 1,786 BC
Hyksos people from the north invade.	1,786 BC
New Kingdom. Amenhotep IV becomes king (1367).	1,567– 1,085 BC
Rameses III fights off invasions by Sea Peoples.	1,179 BC
The Late Dynastic Period. Libyan and Nubian pharaohs rule.	1,085– 332 BC
Egypt becomes part of the Roman Empire.	30 BC

Egypt united

The earliest peoples of Egypt were desert nomads. As they settled and grew to be farmers, they built villages and towns. By 3100 BC, Egypt had become one country. The southern kingdom of Upper Egypt conquered the northern kingdom of Lower Egypt, and King Menes made Memphis his capital.

The Egyptians regarded their king as a god. Thirty dynasties (ruling families) of these god-kings ruled from the time of King Menes in 3100 BC until 332 BC when Alexander the Great conquered Egypt. From about 1554 BC, the Egyptian kings were given the title pharaoh.

△ This picture shows a pharaoh firing an arrow from his battle chariot. It is part of a decorative scene on the side of a chest found in the tomb of the boy-king Tutankhamun.

▷The Nile not only provided Egypt's people with rich, fertile soil and plentiful water but it was also a source of food. Egyptians caught river fish to add to their basic diet. They used spears to hunt ducks on the river too.

△ The shaduf was a bucket swung from the end of a counterweighted pole. It was used to lift water from irrigation ditches, and is still used in Egypt today.

Government and daily life

Egypt was governed by officials and tax collectors, who measured the Nile's waters to predict how high it would flood each year. They could then determine how big a harvest was to be expected. Taxes were set accordingly. Most Egyptians were farmers. They grew crops of barley, wheat, fruit, and vegetables. Their diet consisted of daily meals of bread and beer, often supplemented with fish. Meat from cattle, sheep, and goats was a luxury.

Children began work at the age of five. Boys went to school if their parents could afford to spare them from work, and some girls did too. There were many slaves, but even freemen might be forced to dig irrigation canals or haul stones to building sites. Skilled workers, such as scribes (writers), stone-cutters, carpenters, metalworkers, painters, potters, bakers, and brewers, were kept busy in the towns.

The Egyptians were good at math, particularly at geometry, which they used in architecture and surveying. They drew up an accurate 12-month calendar of 365 days and used water clocks to measure time.

Picture-writing

Egyptian picture-writing is known as hieroglyphics. It was made up of about 750 signs, with pictures of people, animals, and objects. Scribes used a quick form of writing called hieratic.

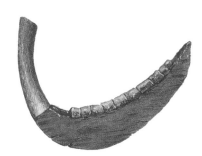

△ Egyptian farmers used sickles to harvest their crops. The harvest period traditionally lasted from March to July. Other farm equipment included ox-drawn wooden plows which were used to prepare the soil before planting time.

BC

400,000

100,000

20,000

10,000

4,000

2,000

Religion played an important part in Egyptian life. The Egyptians believed in many gods and goddesses. Their chief deities were Ra the sun god, Horus the sky god, Osiris the god of the underworld, and Isis, wife of Osiris, who represented the ideal woman.

Pyramids and Gods

This large group of gods was challenged on only one occasion, when the pharaoh Amenhotep tried to introduce worship of one supreme being, the sun god Aton.

Town gods and temples

Gods looked after every aspect of life. Every town and city had its own god, too. Temples were dedicated to a particular god or a dead pharaoh. The biggest of all these temples was the temple of Amun (a sun god who came to be linked with Ra) at Karnak. The pharaoh was the chief priest as well as a god himself. Priests in each temple cared for the statue of the god that was kept there, washing it and offering it gifts of food. Priests also prayed to the gods. Ordinary people said their prayers in the home.

The next world and mummies

The Egyptians believed in an afterlife, to which human souls journeyed after death. They thought it important that the bodies of the dead be preserved for life in the next world, so they developed techniques for making "mummies."

The dead person's organs were removed and the body was embalmed and dried,

First "step" pyramid at Saqqara, built by Imhotep for the pharaoh Zoser.	2,780 BC
Great Pyramid at Giza built for the pharaoh Cheops (Khufu).	2,700 BC
The pharaohs stop building pyramids. Later kings are buried in rock tombs.	1,700 BC
Start of reign of pharaoh Amenhotep III — a great age for Egypt.	1,420 BC
Temples at Luxor built.	1,400 BC
Reign of Amenhotep IV who tries to introduce the worship of one sun god.	1,367 BC
Tutankhamun rules. Egypt returns to the old gods.	1,347 BC
Temples at Abu Simbel are built during the reign of Rameses II.	1,280 BC

▷ The Great Sphinx is a mysterious rock sculpture, with a human head on the body of a lion. Some historians believe it is older than the Pyramids.

34

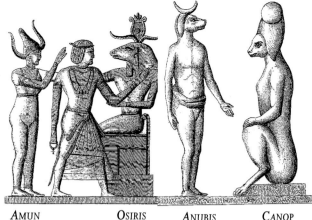

▷ Many Egyptian gods were pictured with animal heads. Horus, son of Isis and Osiris, was shown with a falcon's head. Anubis, god of death, had the head of a jackal.

ISIS   AMUN   OSIRIS   ANUBIS   CANOP

using salts and chemicals, and wrapped in linen bandages. It was then placed in a coffin. Even animals such as cats and monkeys were sometimes mummified. Many thousands of mummies must have been made, but only about 1,000 survive today.

Pyramids and rock tombs

Pyramids are the oldest stone structures in the world. There are more than 30, but the most famous are the three Great Pyramids at Giza. The biggest, which was built for the pharaoh Cheops, contains about 2 million blocks of limestone and is 460 feet high.

The pyramids were built as tombs, to keep the body of the dead king safe for eternity and perhaps (through their sky-pointing shape) to ease his passage to the heavens. The work of building such enormous monuments must have taken years, even with as many as 100,000 workers toiling to move the huge stone blocks up sloping ramps of sand.

Mighty as they were, the pyramids could not keep human robbers out. The treasures left inside each burial chamber with the king were invariably stolen.

△ The sun god Ra was often portrayed simply as a sun disk. He appeared in other forms too, including a cat, a bird, and a lion.

Tutankhamun

Tutankhamun became king of Egypt at the age of 9 and died when he was about 18. His tomb is one of more than 60 royal tombs around the Valley of the Kings. Its four rooms contained more than 5,000 objects – from ostrich feathers and model ships to a throne and a gold death mask.

△ Osiris, god of the dead, was often shown as a mummy on a throne, wearing the crown of Upper Egypt.

BC/AD

Abraham was the founder of the Hebrew people, according to the Bible. In about 1850 BC, he lived in the Sumerian city of Ur. Forced to leave his homeland because of unrest and war, he led his family northeast along the course of the Euphrates, and then west to settle in the land of Canaan.

The Jews

Abraham journeys to Canaan.	1,850 BC
Probable date of Exodus from Egypt.	1,250 BC
Philistines conquer Israel.	1,050 BC
Saul chosen as king.	1,020 BC
King David unites the people. His son Solomon builds the Temple in Jerusalem.	1,010 BC
After the death of Solomon, ten northern tribes break away.	938 BC
Babylonians conquer Judah.	604 BC
Romans conquer Judah.	63 BC
Temple in Jerusalem is destroyed.	AD 66

The Bible records that Abraham had two sons, Ishmael (the ancestor of the Arabs) and Isaac. Isaac had two sons, Esau and Jacob, and Jacob (also called Israel) had 12 sons. These sons became the heads of the Twelve Tribes, the Israelites of the Bible.

Exile in Egypt and Moses

One of Jacob's sons, Joseph, led the Israelites into Egypt after famine struck the land of Canaan. The Israelites became wealthy and influential, but under the rule of successive Egyptian pharaohs, the Israelites were forced into slavery. This slavery lasted until about 1250 BC, when Moses was commanded by God to lead the Israelites out of Egypt in what became known as the Exodus.

Moses was the great law-giver of Jewish history and religion. Jews believe that he received the Ten Commandments from God and taught his people to believe in one God. This belief in one God became the central pillar of the Jewish faith (and later of Christianity and Islam). Moses led the Israelites through the desert to Canaan, where they settled with the local Canaanites and Philistines. For a time,

▷ In this dramatic picture, the Israelites conquer the city of Jericho; at God's command the walls tumble down at the sound of the Israelite army shouting and banging drums.

▷ Moses, the leader of the Hebrew people, receives the two tablets from God. The stone tablets bear the Ten Commandments, as described in the Old Testament. They became the basis for Jewish law.

△ Jews believe that the Dome of the Rock, in Jerusalem, is built over the rock on which Abraham, on God's orders, prepared to sacrifice his son Isaac. Muslims believe that Muhammad rose to heaven from the same rock.

chosen men and women called *judges* led the tribes, but in about 1020 BC, the judge Samuel chose Saul to be the first king of Israel.

Israel and Judah

The Israelites settled in the hills of Canaan. The towns were held by their enemies, the Canaanites and Philistines. The Israelites, under King David, defeated the Philistines. After the death of Solomon, David's son, the kingdom split. Two southern tribes formed their own kingdom, Judah. The northern kingdom of Israel was more powerful but was weakened by royal squabbles and fierce religious disputes. The Assyrians overran Israel in 721 BC. It was crushed by Babylon in 604 BC, and most of the people were taken as slaves.

Exile and conquest

During this exile in Babylon, much of the Bible (Old Testament) took on the form it takes today. In 538 BC, the Persian king Cyrus, conqueror of Babylon, allowed the exiles to leave. Later, Judah became part of the Greek Empire. In 63 BC, the Romans conquered Judah, calling it Judea. In AD 66, the Jews rose in revolt, and the Romans retaliated by destroying the Temple.

King Solomon

Solomon was the son of David, the greatest Israelite king who ruled from 1010 to 970 BC. David defeated the Philistines and enlarged the kingdom, making Jerusalem his capital city. Solomon saw to the building of the Temple in Jerusalem, the most sacred place of the Jewish religion. After Solomon's death Israel split into two separate kingdoms.

△ The Dead Sea scrolls are ancient documents written on leather and copper. They contain the oldest known handwritten texts of books of the Bible.

BC

2,000 1,800 1,600 1,400 1,200 1,000 800 600 400 200 1

The Phoenicians lived along the shores of the eastern Mediterranean (roughly where Lebanon is today). They were the most famous seamen of the ancient world. From 1,200 BC, Phoenicians made trade voyages across the Mediterranean and set up colonies as far away as Morocco and Spain.

Phoenicia and Assyria

The Phoenicians built strong, single-masted ships with one large sail and oars for use in windless conditions or river estuaries. When in unfamiliar territory, the Phoenicians would anchor offshore, land, and set out their goods in "silent trade" with local people.

Assyria independent under King Shamshi-Adad.	1,810 BC
Assyrian power great, then declines.	1,230s BC
Rise of Phoenicians. Tyre is an important city.	1,200 BC
First Phoenician colony in North Africa, at Utica.	1,140 BC
Assyrian power recovers. They conquer Babylon.	1,116 BC
Rise of Carthage.	750 BC
Assyrians attack Babylon.	729 BC
Sargon II starts to build palace at Khorsabad.	721 BC
End of Assyrian Empire.	612 BC
Nineveh destroyed by Medes, Babylonians, and Scythians.	609 BC

The Phonecians' voyages took them beyond the Mediterranean, into the Atlantic Ocean. As explorers and traders, they helped to spread geographical and scientific knowledge. Their fleet was a powerful war weapon, and Phoenician ships were hired by the Persians to attack Greece.

Phoenician colonies

The most famous Phoenician colony was Carthage, in North Africa. Founded some time before 750 BC, Carthage was one of the great cities of the ancient world, with a harbor big enough for hundreds of ships. Its downfall came after a series of wars against the Greeks and final defeat by the Romans in the Punic Wars (264–146 BC).

▷ A Phoenician trading ship at a Mediterranean port. On the dockside, a scribe records the shipment as jars of oil, dye, and textiles are unloaded. In the background is a war galley with oars and a ram for attacking enemy ships.

Ashurbanipal

From 668 to 627 BC, Assyria was ruled by a king called Ashurbanipal. He was the last great Assyrian ruler. Ashurbanipal made the city of Nineveh his capital. Here, he oversaw the building of a magnificent palace and library and ornate gardens.

△ The Phoenicians were famous for their red-purple textiles. They used a dye extracted from mollusks. The name "Phoenician" comes from a Greek word meaning red-purple.

The Assyrians

The Assyrians lived in the northern part of Mesopotamia (what is now northern Iraq). Their homeland was around the upper Tigris River. They were farmers who dug irrigation ditches to water their crops, the most important of which was barley. Numbers of people roamed the land more or less as bandits, and many more fought as soldiers. The Assyrians were feared throughout the Middle East as conquerors.

The rise of the Assyrians began in the 1800s BC. They expanded their trade networks as far as the Mediterranean, but were checked by the strength of the Babylonian king Hammurabi. By about 800 BC, they had a formidable army of cavalry, infantry, and archers. The Assyrians were expert at capturing towns, using wooden siege towers from which to scale or batter down the walls. They earned a reputation for extreme cruelty, slaughtering captives and looting from the peoples they defeated.

The Assyrian chief god was Assur, and the king was Assur's representative on Earth. The king was in charge of the army and the government, and he also controlled the temples and their priests. The Assyrians built on an impressive scale, constructing magnificent temples and palaces in cities such as Assur and Nineveh. Their greatest building was probably the citadel of King Sargon II, in Khorsabad, built in late 700 BC.

◁ Assyrian artists made wall relief sculptures showing winged spirits, hunting scenes, lions, and bulls. For sport, the Assyrian king and his nobles would kill captive lions released into special enclosures.

BC

400,000
100,000
2,000
20,000
4,000
10,000

People had already lived in China for at least 500,000 years when farming began in the valleys of the Huang He (Yellow) and other rivers, more than 5,000 years ago.

China's Early Rulers

From a hazy mixture of history and legend, we learn that China's first ruling family was the Hsia. The legendary first emperors are said to have tamed the rivers, so that farmers could grow millet and wheat.

First farming villages in river valleys.	*c.* 3,000 BC
Traditional date for the discovery of silk by the wife of a Chinese emperor.	2,690 BC
Legendary dynasty of Hsia.	2,200 BC
China's first kings, the Shang. Use of bronze tools.	1,500 BC
The city of Anyang becomes the capital of China.	1,500 BC
Zhou dynasty.	1,122 BC
Period of unrest and civil wars.	770 BC
First emperor, Shih Huang-di of the Qin.	221 BC
Work starts on Great Wall to keep out the Hsiung-nu (Huns).	214 BC

The first rulers known from archaeological evidence were the Shang. From about 1500 BC, they controlled the best farmland around the Huang He valley, and from there their power spread.

Shang slendor
The Shang kings were cruel, ruling in barbaric splendor. They built China's first cities. Shang bronzesmiths were experts at making cooking pots, tools, and weapons. Slave workers sweated to dig enormous pit tombs for dead kings, who were buried with treasures, chariots, and horses, and dozens of slain servants and soldiers to accompany their master into the next world. Farmers supplied food to the local nobleman, in return for protection.

The Zhou invaders
Shang rule lasted until 1122 BC. By then, according to Chinese history, the rulers had become tyrants. The Zhou from the west invaded and overthrew the last

▷ Ordinary people lived in villages, growing grains and raising chickens, pigs, sheep, and cattle. They used oxen and water buffalo to pull plows and dug ditches to water their fields.

△ *Fierce warriors helped to keep the Shang rulers, China's first dynasty, in power for more than 400 years.*

△ *This food vessel, from the time of the Shang dynasty, is decorated with intricate animal motifs. It is in the form of a tiger protecting the body of a man.*

Chinese writing

An example of Chinese writing on silk. The Chinese wrote in picture signs and made up about 50,000 characters. The first important work of Chinese literature, a collection of poems, dates from before 1000 BC.

Shang king. The new kings were backed by powerful nobles. Nobles built forts and walled towns to defend their lands against one another. They also fought off fierce nomads who swept down from the northern steppes on sturdy horses.

Warring states

No Zhou ruler was strong enough to control all China. For 500 years, small warring states fought for power. Yet China still prospered. Farmers grew more food, and metalworkers mastered the new skills of making iron tools. Potters, jewelers, tailors, and chariot-makers were kept busy. Scholars attended the nobles' courts, seeking work as government officials. Trade grew, and people began to use money.

The first emperor

The Qin ruler Shih Huang-di fought his way to power as first emperor of all China in 221 BC. He crushed the power of the nobles, handing over the government to hired officials (who did what he told them). He ordered everyone to speak the same language and to use the same weights and measures. Thousands of people were forced to build new roads and canals, and the emperor also built the Great Wall, which linked up older walls to create the biggest frontier defense on the earth.

◁ *The Shang kings were superstitious. They consulted "oracle bones" before making any important decisions. A soothsayer would read the signs in animal bones cracked by heat, and advise the king accordingly.*

BC

400,000

100,000

20,000

10,000

4,000

2,000

War has been a part of life for as long as humans have existed. Prehistoric people fought for territory and food, using rocks and sticks as weapons. Later, they used stone-tipped spears and bows and arrows.

War and Weapons

The discovery of bronze in about 3500 BC brought the first revolution in weaponry. Bronze swords and spear points were sharper than stone and bone weapons. Iron was even stronger still. Peoples of the Near East, such as the Hittites, were the first to master iron-making.

Armies and armor

Each of the ancient Near East superpowers rounded up civilians to serve in armies for the conquest of other countries, and for defense against enemies. To protect themselves, soldiers began wearing armor on their bodies. By the time of the Trojan War, about 1200 BC, armor was made from metal plates fastened with leather thongs. Soldiers

A sculpture shows an Egyptian king pictured defeating an enemy.	3,100 BC
Sumerians make bronze war axes and spear points.	2,500 BC
Body armor used by Egyptians and Mesopotamians.	2,000 BC
Chariots in use in Egypt and Near East. Sickle-shaped swords of bronze.	1,500 BC
First iron swords. End of Trojan War.	1,200 BC
Assyrian armies include infantry, cavalry, and chariots.	800 BC
Chainmail made from iron links replaces bronze armor.	500 BC
Sparta has the first full-time army in the Greek world.	400s BC

▷Assyrian troops used wheeled siege towers with iron-tipped rams to batter down the walls of enemy towns.

△ Egyptian soldiers fought with *spears, axes, clubs, javelins (throwing spears), swords, and bows and arrows. Trumpeters blew signal calls to direct the troops.*

△ *Axe heads were made from bronze (shown here) and iron. A popular weapon, particularly among Chinese troops, was a halberd, a long spear with an axelike head.*

Hittite charioteers

The Hittites, a fierce people from Anatolia (modern Turkey), were the first to use chariots in war. Hittite archers fired their arrows from these chariots, giving them a great advantage over the enemy.

wore metal helmets to protect the head, and carried shields (usually round or rectangular). Some warriors scorned armor – the Greeks and Celts sometimes fought practically naked.

The first organized armies

Kings had small bodyguards of trained soldiers, including chariot-drivers, but they still relied on untrained peasants as foot soldiers. The Assyrians organized the first "professional" army, and were greatly feared because of its ferocity. An Assyrian army included cavalry (soldiers on horses) and infantry (soldiers on foot).

Assyrian soldiers wore chainmail armor and fought with iron swords and spears. Archers rode into battle on chariots, then sheltered behind basketwork shields to fire and reload. Slingers hurled stones, often farther than a javelin.

Infantry and cavalry

In China, soldiers traditionally fought on foot and in huge armies (as many as 100,000 men). Facing marauders on horseback, the Chinese had to become horse-soldiers too. The Chinese composite bow of wood and bone had a longer range than a simple bow. Chinese archers also used crossbows.

There was the clash of shields, of spears and the fury of men cased in bronze... then there were mingled the groaning and the crowing of men killed and killing.

from THE ILIAD, HOMER (8TH CENTURY BC)

Nothing is known about Homer for certain. Tradition states he lived near Greece and wrote two great poems about the Trojan wars: The Iliad *and* The Odyssey.

BC

Rivers and lakes in Sahara start to dry up as climate changes.	3,500 BC
Origins of Kush.	2,000 BC
Sahara is a desert. Egyptians invade Kush.	1,500 BC
Iron-working in northern Africa.	1,000 BC
Traditional date for founding of Carthage.	814 BC
Kush throws off Egyptian rule. Kushites conquer Egypt.	750 BC
Nok culture in West Africa. Iron-working spreads into east Africa.	500 BC
Kushite city of Meroe at its finest.	300 BC

Other civilizations of Africa were developing to the south of Egypt. These peoples traded with the land of the pharaohs and with each other along the rivers and across the mighty Sahara Desert.

African Civilizations

Before 6000 BC, the Sahara had a wetter climate than now. The herders and hunters who lived among its lakes left rock paintings showing a Saharan grassland and wildlife very different from the desert of today. About 3500 BC, the Sahara began to dry up, but people still followed old trade routes across the spreading desert.

A network of trade routes linked the peoples of West Africa with others in the Nile Valley and in North Africa. In Africa, the Stone Age and Iron Age overlapped. Herders became ironsmiths, moving with their herds and tools and spreading the use of iron across Africa.

Kingdom of Kush

The kingdom of Kush was in Nubia (modern Sudan). It lay in the shadow of Egypt and was at first ruled by Egyptians. Its chief cities were Napata on the River Nile, and later Meroe, a city which grew in importance because iron was mined close by. Meroe was impressive, with stone and brick palaces, baths, and the temple of the Kush lion-god Apedemeck. Kushite kings were buried in pyramid-shaped tombs beside the Nile.

△ Many of the African kingdoms and peoples traded with the Egyptians to the north. Egyptian traders wanted copper, ivory and ebony, animal skins, cattle, and slaves. They paid for these goods with gold, barley, wheat, and papyrus.

△ *A section of a wall painting from a tomb of ancient Egypt. It shows a group of Nubians offering various gifts to the Egyptian pharaoh.*

Carthage

The city-state of Carthage had two large harbors, crammed with naval and trading vessels. It was overlooked by the Byrsa, a huge walled fortress on the hill above.

The Nok people

South and west of the great desert, trade caravans carrying salt and slaves across the Sahara gathered at small towns. The market towns grew into cities and some, such as Djenne in Mali, still thrive.

The Niger River valley was the home of the Nok people. Their society developed from about 500 BC. Most people were farmers, but others were merchants, ironsmiths, and craftworkers. Each town had its own king. He ruled over a community of large family groups, in which three or four generations lived together. Temples honored ancestors and heroes. Nok artists made elegant clay heads and figures of people.

The city-state of Carthage

Before the rise of Rome, the city-state of Carthage, in what is now Tunisia, ruled the Mediterranean. Traditionally founded in 814 BC by Phoenicians from Tyre, Carthage grew rich on trade.

The Carthaginians were daring seamen, sailing their oared ships across the Mediterranean and into the Atlantic. An explorer named Hanno is said to have sailed as far south as the Guinea coast of West Africa. Carthage remained rich and powerful for 600 years, until it challenged Rome in three costly wars and lost.

Carthage had wealth and power; and it had skill and ferocity in war. Juno is said to have loved Carthage best of all cities in the world.

THE AENEID, VIRGIL (70-19 BC)

Virgil's Aeneid tells the story of Aeneas, who visited Carthage before he founded the city of Rome.

△ *Nok sculptures are made of terracotta, a kind of earthenware. Some are life-size. There are figures of people, animals, and heads.*

The first people to settle the Americas, crossed from Asia and lived as wandering hunters or settled along the coasts in fishing communities. Groups of people traveled farther south, through the forests and prairies, across the jungles and mountains of Panama, and into the grasslands, rainforests, and mountains of South America.

The Americas

Many of these first settlers of the Americas continued to live as hunter-gatherers. Some became farmers and settled in villages which grew into towns. Two groups developed the Americas earliest civilizations – in Mesoamerica (Mexico and Central America) and in Peru on the west coast of South America.

The Olmecs of Mesoamerica

The Olmecs flourished between about 1200 and 400 BC. They made pottery and cleared the jungle to grow crops. They traveled along rivers on rafts and canoes and settled near rivers. These villages grew to become the first towns in Mexico and Central America. The Olmecs believed in nature gods of the forest and of fertility, and in their towns, they built earth mounds with straw and mud temples on top to worship these gods.

Farmers grew corn, chilis, beans, and squash. People also collected shellfish and hunted forest animals with spears and nets. Olmec society was ruled by a small group of priest-nobles, who carried out temple ceremonies, owned the best farmland, and controlled trade in valuable raw materials, such as jade.

Stone Age hunters move into the Andes Mountains.	8,000 BC
People in Peru grow beans, corn, and other crops.	7,000 BC
Cotton weaving begins in Peru.	2,500 BC
First Mayan languages – in Mexico.	.2,500 BC
Religious centers, with stone temples, built in Peru.	2,000 BC
First use of iron in South America.	c. 1,500 BC
Growth of settlements in Olmec region.	1,200–900 BC
Rise of Chavin civilization.	1,000 BC
Gold-working is widespread in South America.	800 BC

▷ The Olmec people constructed large stepped pyramids from earth. They held religious ceremonies and worshiped their gods in temples built on top of these pyramids.

▷ In modern Peru, craftworkers carry on the traditions of their Chavin ancestors, producing colorful handwoven textiles. Designs such as these have been produced in Peru for approximately 3,000 years.

Stone heads and sacrifices

The most remarkable Olmec remains are huge stone heads, some 6.5 feet high, and other carvings of human figures with flattened features. They may represent human sacrifices. Prisoners taken in war, or contestants in a ritual ball game, may have been killed as sacrifices to the Olmec jaguar-god. Carvings show priests wearing jaguar masks. Some symbols cut into stones may be numbers, suggesting the Olmecs had a calendar.

Civilizations of Peru

In South America, people living in the Andes foothills had become farmers by about 1000 BC. They built the first towns in South America. One of the earliest civilizations of the Andes was Chavin de Huantar in Peru.

Like the Olmecs, the Chavins were ruled by priests, who later became nobles serving a king. They set up rows of stone pillars that look like ceremonial routes. They also carved stone heads and sculptures of jaguars, snakes, and condors. The Chavins used wool from alpacas and vicuñas to weave textiles. Although they had only stone tools, they made beautiful gold, silver, and copper jewelery.

△ The mysterious stone head sculptures made by the Olmecs may have been totems, made to protect the people from enemies or natural disaster. Using stone chisels and hammers, the Olmec people worked on their sculptures in teams.

Chavin farmers

The Chavin people grew corn, potatoes, and peppers. They cut terraces into hillsides and became expert at irrigation (channeling water) to cultivate the dry land and mountain slopes. Families kept llamas, guinea pigs, and dogs for meat.

△ An Olmec figurine carved from jade. Skilled craftworkers made carvings and sculptures from stone, clay, and jade.

Index

RIDEAU CENTENNIAL SCHOOL
Portland, Ontario